HENDRIX
STILL BURNING BRIGHT

Publisher's Note: Readers will note that the sharpness of the images in this book varies. This is to be expected of photography from this era and of this nature. Images have been chosen not just for their quality, but also for their intimacy and evocative insight into Jimi Hendrix's history.

Publisher and Creative Director: Nick Wells

Commissioning Editor: Polly Prior

Art Director & Layout Design: Mike Spender

Digital Design & Production: Chris Herbert

Special thanks to: Karen Fitzpatrick, Dawn Laker and Catherine Taylor

FLAME TREE PUBLISHING

6 Melbray Mews, Fulham,

London SW6 3NS, United Kingdom

www.flametreepublishing.com

First published 2020

20 22 24 23 21

1 3 5 7 9 10 8 6 4 2

© 2020 Flame Tree Publishing Ltd

ISBN: 978-1-83964-220-3

A CIP record for this book is available from the British Library.

Printed in China | Created, Developed & Produced in the United Kingdom

HENDRIX
STILL BURNING BRIGHT

HUGH FIELDER
FOREWORD BY PAUL DU NOYER

FLAME TREE
PUBLISHING

Contents

Foreword

The fingers probably helped, of course. They stretched so far, somebody said, that his hands looked like those of a man twelve inches taller. But his graceful way around a guitar neck was only part of whatever magic made Jimi Hendrix into a star.

We find so many things combined inside his slender frame: the musical virtuoso, the gifted songwriter, the singer with such emotional range. Supremely stylish too, and even a sex god. When this unknown young American hit the British pop scene in 1967, it came as a seismic shock to everyone from the Beatles downwards.

Nobody had sounded like this before. Nobody had looked like this before. Lightning had struck in London and nothing in rock could ever be the same. Even at a time of wild innovation, Jimi Hendrix was mind-scrambling. The reigning local guitar hero, Eric Clapton, watched with awe. As Bing Crosby had said of his rival Frank Sinatra: 'An artist like this only comes around once in a lifetime. But why did it have to be *my* lifetime?'

It was utterly unforeseeable. Hendrix brought a lifetime's understanding of black American music to the acid dandyism of Swinging England. It was blues, science fiction and cosmic voodoo. He had Afro hair and psychedelic clothes, a soulman's raunch but a poet's sensitivity. He was cool as jazz itself, but made the pop kids love him. It was dazzling but it was full of feeling too. It was a glorious noise and may it never be silenced.

Paul Du Noyer

Man + Guitar

Jimi Hendrix is the most innovative and influential rock guitarist who has ever lived. He changed the way the electric guitar was played, transforming its possibilities and its image. Hendrix pioneered the guitar as an electronic sound source. Other guitarists had toyed with feedback and distortion, but Hendrix turned these and other effects into a controlled, personalized sound that generations of guitarists since have followed and embellished.

Left-handed View

Hendrix was left-handed and played his favourite guitar, a Fender Stratocaster, upside down and re-strung. This gave him a different perspective on the instrument and an alternative view of the Fender's tremolo arm, which enabled him to bend notes and chords without the strings going out of tune.

He never stopped looking for ways to get new sounds out of the guitar – from within the instrument itself, toying with the tension springs, to electronic gadgets he could connect to it, like the

Monterey Pop Festival, June 1967

'Technically I'm not a guitar player, all I play is truth and emotion.'

JIMI HENDRIX

wah-wah pedal. In the studio he was particularly alert to using new and experimental recording techniques.

'You either have the magic or you don't. There's no way you can work up to it. There's nobody who can take his place.'

FREDDIE MERCURY

Guitar Love Affair

From the moment he started playing, in his hometown of Seattle, Washington, Hendrix was never more than a few feet from a guitar. Virtually everyone who met him remarks that he almost always had a guitar to hand, even musicians that he met only briefly. Girlfriends also confirm that he took it to bed with him.

The Speakeasy, London, January 1967

From Introvert To Extrovert

Offstage, Hendrix was quiet, softly spoken, unassuming with a dry wit that was often self-deprecating. He seemed unaware of his own charisma. Onstage, however, he was transformed. His antics were as flamboyant as his clothes. He would coax sounds out of his guitar by grinding it against the speakers or rubbing it against a microphone stand. He would play the guitar behind his head, he would play it with his teeth, he would lick the strings. On occasion he even sacrificed his guitar by ritually burning it. He could also be sexually suggestive on stage, flicking his tongue at girls in the audience, thrusting his hips at his guitar. But it was all done with passion and showmanship, rather than aggression. Hendrix had an intense relationship with his playing and his music; it was at the core of his charisma and his genius.

Iconic Sixties Superstar

More than a guitarist or a performer, Hendrix was a superstar. He played to millions of people and sold millions more records. He wrote classic rock songs like 'Purple Haze', 'Voodoo Child (Slight Return)', 'The Wind Cries Mary' and 'Little Wing', which were not just superb showcases for his guitar but were hugely popular, appealing to people who didn't know or care whether his guitar was upside down or not. And although he never regarded himself as a singer, his natural, intimate style was often as evocative as his playing, adding to his broad appeal.

'Music doesn't lie. If there is something to be changed in this world, then it can only happen through music.'

JIMI HENDRIX

Above all, Hendrix remains an iconic image of the Sixties. His wild frizzy hair, florid clothes and soft, sensuous features are symbolic of those mind-expanding times. It has never been uncool to have an image of Hendrix on your T-shirt.

Who Was Jimi Hendrix?

Hendrix would never have achieved the success he did if he had not come to the UK. There was no hint that his talent was recognized, let alone encouraged or developed, before he left the US for the UK in September 1966.

musician touring the so-called 'Chitlin' Circuit' (a network of clubs in black neighbourhoods across the southern United States) in a variety of bands before arriving in New York. There was no such racial divide in the British music industry. The scene had been blown open by the Beatles and the Rolling

'We call our music electric church music, because it's like a religion to us.'

JIMI HENDRIX

Born in America, Made in England

The black and white music industries in the United States in the 1960s were almost entirely separate, catering for their respective audiences. Hendrix had spent his early years as a

Receiving 'World's Best Musician' award, London, September 1967

Stones, followed by the likes of The Who and The Animals, and was far more receptive to new sounds and ideas, both of which Hendrix had in abundance.

Short and Sweet

Hendrix's career was remarkably brief. Throughout 1967 and 1968, his rise was meteoric, first in the UK and then in the US. During this time, he released the three albums on which his

legend is based – *Are You Experienced*, *Axis: Bold As Love* and *Electric Ladyland*. In 1969 and 1970, he gradually came to terms with his musical reputation and fame and was looking for a new musical direction to follow.

In total he released just five albums while he was alive, and one of those was a greatest hits compilation. He was preparing to release a new album when he died of an accidental overdose of sleeping pills in London in September 1970. He was 27 years old and became an early member of the phenomenon that was

Graffiti, 'The 27 Club', Tel Aviv

later known as the Forever 27 Club, consisting of rock stars who all died at that age. Fellow members include Brian Jones (1969), Janis Joplin (1970), Jim Morrison (1971), Kurt Cobain (1994) and Amy Winehouse (2011).

Uneasy Afterlife

After Hendrix's premature death, a series of hastily compiled albums featuring unreleased songs – many of them unfinished

'He played his own s**t, he didn't play nobody else's stuff like they do now. Jimi was original.'

ALBERT COLLINS

– began to erode his reputation, along with a growing number of pre-1967 recordings that erroneously claimed to feature Hendrix. Although he never lost his genius-like status among musicians, his public image declined during the Seventies and Eighties as music fashions changed.

In the late Eighties, his public reputation revived and was given a major boost in the early Nineties when Wrangler Jeans used his song 'Crosstown Traffic' in a TV commercial and introduced his music to a new generation.

The Legacy

It is impossible to say how Hendrix's career might have progressed if he had lived and it is pointless to speculate. The music that he was working on at the time of his death shows that he was in something of a transitional phase, moving on from the music and the extrovert performing style with which he had established his superstar status, but with no clear new direction evident. He had been taking a keen interest in the musical developments around him, including jazz, and he was particularly interested in the recent albums by Miles Davis. However, the music that he left behind has ensured that the legend remains undiminished 50 years later and will remain so.

'Jimi Hendrix is … my idol. He … epitomizes, from his presentation on stage, the whole works of a rock star.'

FREDDIE MERCURY

Royal Albert Hall, February 1969

1942-61: Voodoo Chile

Jimi Hendrix was born on 27 November 1942 in Seattle, Washington. He was named Johnny Allen Hendrix by his mother, Lucille, who was 17 years old and of Cherokee Indian descent. His father, 23-year-old Al Hendrix, was not present at the birth. He had been denied permission to leave the army camp in Alabama where he was stationed.

Seattle Days

Al Hendrix had grown up in Vancouver, Canada, the son of vaudeville performers. He had been a tap dancer for a while, before moving down to Seattle and getting a factory job. When he first met Lucille she was a local jitterbug champion, and for their first date he took her to see Fats Waller, the legendary pianist and entertainer, best known for his Thirties' hits 'Ain't Misbehavin'' and 'Honeysuckle Rose'. Lucille was 16 when they got married.

JH (aged 3) with father, Al Hendrix, 1945

When Al was granted leave to return to Seattle, he found that Lucille was farming baby Johnny out to friends and relatives while she resumed a carefree existence. Al was not best pleased, although they later got back together again. Al renamed his son James Marshall Hendrix in 1946 – something about the name Johnny irked him.

'Lord, I'm a voodoo chile / Well, the night I was born / Lord, I swear the moon turned a fire red.' JIMI HENDRIX

Family Life

Jimmy's parents' marriage remained volatile, although Jimmy was joined by a younger brother, Leon, in 1948. His mother would often disappear for days on end and the only settled period of his childhood he could recall was the summer of 1949 when he stayed with Al's sister in Vancouver. His parents finally divorced in 1951 when he was eight. His brother Leon was fostered out several times, but Jimmy stayed with his father,

Mickey & Sylvia, c. 1958

moving house several times during the mid-1950s as Al changed jobs. Not surprisingly, he was a somewhat withdrawn child at the succession of different schools he attended.

His earliest musical exposure came from his father's records – jazz by Duke Ellington and Count Basie, R&B by Louis Jordan and Big Joe Turner. The first pop record he could remember was the 1956 hit by Mickey & Sylvia 'Love Is Strange', with its distinctive guitar riff and clever vocal interplay.

'I learned to play on a guitar which belonged to one of my father's friends who came to play cards.'

JIMI HENDRIX

First Guitar

Jimmy showed enough musical interest – graduating from a piece of string and a broom handle to an elastic band stretched over a cigar box – for Al to find a one-string ukulele for him. But the tipping point came when he went to see Elvis Presley in 1957. He watched Elvis ride on stage in a Cadillac and, at the end, asking everyone to stand up for the national anthem before singing 'Hound Dog'. The impact was not lost on Jimmy.

His mother's death the following year from a ruptured spleen, caused by damage she had inflicted on her liver, was a traumatic blow. Al wouldn't let Jimmy attend the funeral and his emotions were bottled up. Not long afterwards, Al was offered a guitar for $5 and bought it for Jimmy.

Al Hendrix, c. 1998

'I listen to everything that's written. From rock to The Beatles to Muddy Waters to Elmore James… And I listen to Bob Dylan.'

JIMI HENDRIX

Self-portrait, c. 1966

Early Sounds

Being left-handed he turned it upside down and started to learn how to strum along to records by blues artists like Muddy Waters, Elmore James and Chuck Berry. In 1959, he joined a local band called the Rocking Kings, playing bass and performing covers like 'At The Hop' by Danny & The Juniors, 'Yakety Yak' by the Coasters and 'Sleepwalk' by Santo & Johnny at dance halls and parties. They were good enough to come second in the Washington All State Band of The Year Contest in 1960, but they fell apart after their first attempt to play outside Washington. They reconstituted themselves as Thomas & The Tomcats and this time Jimmy was on guitar.

Around this time, Jimmy enrolled at Garfield High School in Seattle to complete his schooling, but he left in the autumn of 1960 without graduating. He took to hanging around clubs, notably the Spanish Castle, looking for an opportunity to play with almost anyone.

He had the music bug, but it wasn't leading him anywhere and he was arrested twice in three days for taking a car without permission. When the case came to court in May 1961, Jimmy said that he was considering joining the army and was given a two-year suspended sentence.

1962-65: Reluctant Recruit

Jimmy was posted to the 101st Airborne Paratroopers at Fort Campbell, Kentucky, as a member of the elite Screaming Eagles squad. He made 26 parachute jumps, attaining the rank of Private, First Class. He said later that the sound of the air whistling through the parachute suspension lines was one of the main inspirations for the spacey guitar sounds he would produce later.

Army Days

If life at 10,000 feet was exhilarating, however, the discipline at ground level was another matter. At the beginning of 1962, he had his red Danelectro guitar sent to him from Seattle and whiled away the hours lying on his bed playing it. While this might be acceptable student behaviour, it marked him out at army camp, and brought him to the attention of Private Billy Cox, a bass player. It wasn't long before the two of them were

US Army, Fort Campbell, Kentucky, 1960

setting up a band called The King Kasuals (or the Casuals) to play army camps and nearby towns.

'They say it takes 24,000 hours to be proficient with an instrument and I saw him do that in almost five years 'cause it was a night and day affair.'

BILLY COX

They were hatching grander plans when Jimmy broke his ankle on his 26th parachute jump and was considered medically unsuitable to continue. He was given an honourable discharge and then waited for Billy to complete his service.

JH (L) with the Isley Brothers, Rockland Palace, New York, June 1964

'It just seems to me that music has a lot of influence on a lot of young people today, you know.'

JIMI HENDRIX

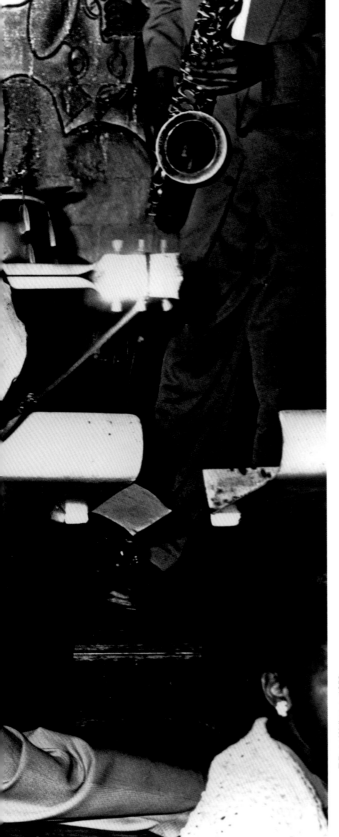

T-Bone Walker, c. 1950

On The Road

The next three years of Jimmy's life are difficult to trace with any accuracy as he became an itinerant musician, travelling around the country. After Billy re-joined him, they moved to Indianapolis and then Nashville. Here, they met another guitarist, Larry Lee, who moved Jimmy's guitar playing on apace and encouraged his innate sense of showmanship.

'I remember my first gig was at an armoury… we earned 35 cents apiece.'

JIMI HENDRIX

Together they made an elongated guitar lead so that Jimmy could walk out into the audience – and sometimes out on to the street from smaller clubs, where they played as Bob Fisher & The Barnevilles. It was a stunt they had picked up from the popular Forties' and Fifties' bluesman T-Bone Walker. Jimmy also copied another of T-Bone's tricks, playing the guitar behind his head.

33

After a stint in Curtis Mayfield's backing band, Jimmy was spotted by band leader and promoter George Odell in early 1963.

'My guitar is my medium, and I want to turn the world on.'

JIMI HENDRIX

The Chitlin' Circuit

This was a chance he had to take, and he split from Billy Cox and Larry Lee, going out on the Chitlin' Circuit – appearing on the same bills as some of the great soul singers like Sam Cooke, Solomon Burke and Jackie Wilson. Jimmy was learning plenty, but the constrictions of life in a band – playing the same songs in the same way every night – was frustrating. There were compensations, however, like meeting blues guitarist Albert King, who gave him advice on playing left-handed. But when another promoter promised him some work in New York, Jimmy again decided to take the chance. En route he stopped off in Philadelphia where he came across Lonnie Youngblood, a saxophone player who was a popular attraction at college dances, and did some recording sessions with him.

Jimmy arrived in New York early in 1964 and settled into Harlem, where he became another musician looking for a break. In March he landed a spot with the Isley Brothers, who were going through a lull after their R&B hits with 'Shout' and 'Twist & Shout'. But they could still pull a crowd, and Jimmy toured the country with them, as well as performing in Canada and Bermuda. This enabled him to update his guitar to a Fender Duo-Sonic. He also played on all their recording sessions during 1964, including on the closest they came to a hit single, 'Testify'. He was credited as Jimmy James, and you can hear him in the mix, showing a good sense of rhythm with a couple of fluid breaks.

The Isley Brothers weren't working continuously, however, so Jimmy found himself back on the Chitlin' Circuit to make ends meet. He was briefly in Sam Cooke's band, leaving just a few weeks before Sam was shot, as well as in Little Richard's band, playing on 'I Don't Know What You've Got But It's Got Me', which was an R&B hit at the end of 1964. The flamboyant Little Richard, however, was not prepared to share his spotlight, and Jimmy did not last long.

1965-66: This Gigging Life

Jimmy's hand-to-mouth existence continued into 1965 and, when he wasn't on tour, he would return to New York, where he would generally find a girlfriend's pad to crash in. It was around this time that he got to know Devon Wilson, an aspiring groupie and confidante whose career would follow a similar trajectory to Jimmy's.

Down And Out In New York City

In the autumn of 1965, he joined singer and guitarist Curtis Knight's band, the Squires. Curtis had a good live reputation and Jimmy had more freedom in his R&B/soul revue than he'd enjoyed in previous bands and Curtis was happy to give him a spot in the show.

'He just took the blues and intensified it.' ETTA JAMES

JH with Curtis Knight & The Squires, c. 1966

JH (left) with Curtis Knight And The Squires, 1966

Curtis also introduced him to his manager and producer Ed Chalpin. As soon as he heard Jimmy, he signed him to an exclusive three-year recording contract for a $1 advance and a 15 per cent royalty. Jimmy's first recording session with Curtis in October produced a track called 'How Would You Feel', a bluesy take on Bob Dylan's 'Like A Rolling Stone'.

'[Jimi and I] were locked together spiritually, and I think that doesn't happen so much nowadays. BILLY COX

Seeking A Breakthrough

Chalpin also recorded Curtis Knight & The Squires live at George's Club 20, Hackensack, New Jersey on Boxing Day 1965 with Jimmy taking the spotlight on several numbers, including his own 'Drivin' South', and demonstrating a forward-looking approach to the blues. His vocal style is raw but already recognizable and he performs cunnilingus on his guitar, prompting shouts of 'Eat it, Jimmy, eat it,' from Curtis. But Curtis Knight could not find that elusive breakthrough hit and in the early part of 1966, Jimmy joined renowned saxophone King Curtis who had played the solo on the Coasters' 'Yakety Yak' as well as having a hit of his own with 'Soul Serenade' in 1964. His band included guitarist Cornell Dupree and drummer Bernard Purdie, both of whom would become top session players over the next decade.

Waiting To Be Found

Jimmy was still hanging around the Greenwich Village clubs, available to fill in whenever an act needed a guitarist at short notice and running into other guitarists like John Hammond Junior, Roy Buchanan and Mike Bloomfield. He also met drummer Buddy Miles who was playing in Wilson Pickett's band and riding the crest of the wave with Wilson's hit, 'In the Midnight Hour'.

In the summer of 1966, Jimmy finally got his own band together, Jimmy James and The Blue Flames, and started playing gigs at Café Wha? and other clubs around the Village. For a while the group included the young Randy California who would go on to form the rock group Spirit. They started

to pick up a buzz among the club regulars, many of whom were musicians.

'... when [Jimi] started playing with his teeth, and behind his head, it was obvious that here was someone different.'

TAPPY WRIGHT (ANIMALS' ROADIE)

At The Café

It was at Café Wha? where Chas Chandler first saw Jimmy. Chas was the bassist in the Animals, the Newcastle band who had scored a No. 1 hit in the UK and US with 'House of the Rising Sun' in 1964, and spearheaded the British invasion of the United States with the Beatles and the Rolling Stones. But by the summer of 1966, the hits had dried up and the

Animals had worked themselves into a state of exhaustion. Chas could see the end was nigh and he needed to re-think his career.

Chas was recommended to check out Jimmy by Linda Keith, girlfriend of Rolling Stones guitarist Keith Richards. She was one of the Café Wha? regulars and had seen Jimmy enough times to know he was something special. Chas reached the same conclusion at first sight and realized that the British rock scene would be a far more receptive place for Jimmy's talent than the US. What swung it was Jimmy's distinctive interpretation of a song that several US acts had picked up on in the past couple of years, 'Hey Joe'.

London-Bound

After the show, he went backstage and made his pitch to Jimmy, offering to take him over to London and launch him in the UK. Jimmy considered his options. There were no other offers, he had no ties, he hadn't been back to Seattle in five years, the only contact he'd made was the occasional postcard. What did he have to lose?

There was a short delay while Jimmy retrieved his birth certificate in order to get his passport. On 23 September 1966, Jimmy and Chas boarded a plane for London.

Linda Keith, 1966

'This is a world of lead guitar players, but the most essential thing to learn is the rhythm, the time.'

JIMI HENDRIX

1966-67: Becoming Experienced

Somewhere on the flight over the Atlantic, Jimmy James changed his name to Jimi Hendrix, not least because there was already a Jimmy James lurking on the British soul scene.

Becoming Jimi

On arrival in London, Jimi was taken to the London home of Zoot Money, a well-known musician on the underground scene. He spent the afternoon jamming with Zoot and later guested with him at The Scotch of St James, a club frequented by musicians and music businesspeople. The buzz was immediate. A week later, Jimi made another guest appearance with the highly touted new rock trio Cream, featuring Eric Clapton, already acclaimed on graffiti as 'God'. Jimi walked on stage at the London Polytechnic and played 'Killing Floor'. Clapton was gobsmacked. The first priority was to find a band for Jimi. The Jimi Hendrix Experience came together quickly, almost intuitively. Mitch Mitchell had

The Speakeasy, London, January 1966

'He did a few of his tricks, like playing with his teeth and behind his back… and my life was never the same again.' ERIC CLAPTON

played with Georgie Fame and was the drummer in the house band for the weekly TV pop show *Ready Steady Go!* He was cocky and brash, not overawed by Jim. Noel Redding was a guitarist who had played in a couple of minor groups and wasn't looking to play bass. But Jimi was looking for a particular kind of bassist. He'd played bass himself and could explain what he was looking for. Noel decided to play bass.

Purple Haze

They released their first single, Jimi's stinging, brooding version of 'Hey Joe' that had so impressed Chas Chandler (who had now gone into partnership with Animals manager Mike Jeffery to fund Jimi's career) just before Christmas 1966. Appearances on the BBC's *Top of The Pops* early in 1967 brought Jimi's extrovert performing style into the nation's living rooms. They also packed out London's premier club, The Marquee, and attracted swinging London to the prestigious Saville Theatre, recently acquired by Beatles manager Brian Epstein.

'Hey Joe' peaked at No. 6 in the UK charts, but it was the follow-up, 'Purple Haze', released in March, that galvanized the entire British music scene. It's hard to overstate the impact of the opening discordant two-note riff and searing guitar riff, propelled by a thudding beat, and Jimi's opening line, 'Purple haze, all in my

The Jimi Hendrix Experience, London, May 1967

brain', followed by a blitz of distortion on the edge of feedback, climaxing with an orgy of wailing whammy bar. Little wonder that it quickly became an anthem for the emerging counterculture.

Burning His Guitar

As 'Purple Haze' blazed its way up to No. 3, Jimi headed out on his first national tour in the unlikely company of headlining crooner Englebert Humperdinck and aspiring pop star Cat Stevens. On the opening night at London's Astoria, Hendrix, resplendent in velvet flares and a military jacket, pulled another stunt. Instigated by Chas Chandler, he set his guitar alight at the end of his set and grabbed all the publicity the next day. Outside London, however, several reviewers complained about Jimi's 'suggestive' antics.

Soundtrack to Summer '67

Jimi's third single, recorded at the same session as 'Purple Haze', was an abrupt change of pace. 'The Wind Cries Mary' was a reflective ballad, proving that Jimi was more than a pyrotechnic guitar hero. His vocals were structured around a simple chord pattern and concise guitar solo, all completed in under 20 minutes, overdubs included.

'[Jimi] was the first guy who wasn't only a pop star, he was a virtuoso musician.'

STING

With Chas Chandler, March 1967

'[Jimi] came walking forward playing "Sgt. Pepper". I put that down as one of the great honours of my career.'

PAUL MCCARTNEY

Any suspicions that Jimi might be going soft were dispelled in May with the release of the first album, *Are You Experienced*, one of the most outstanding debut albums ever released, from the opening lascivious 'Foxy Lady' to the closing, spacey title track. Drawing on a range of styles and influences, Jimi evolved an array of guitar sounds with engineer Eddie Kramer using flanging, double tracking and variable recording speeds, creating noises that could evoke howls of wind or deep space, according to the mood of the song.

It wasn't just the guitar; the combination of Noel's fuzzy, distorted bass and Mitch's trebly, very British drumming added another dimension. To those who were experienced, it was the sound of psychedelia and became an integral soundtrack to the summer of 1967, only kept from the No. 1 spot by the Beatles' *Sgt Pepper's Lonely Hearts Club Band*. To guitarists everywhere, it was (and remains) a life-altering experience.

'Who I am as a guitarist is defined by my failure to become Jimi Hendrix.'

JOHN MAYER

1967: On Fire

Back at London's Saville Theatre in early June, the Jimi Hendrix Experience opened their show with a suitably groovy version of 'Sgt Pepper's Lonely Hearts Club Band' (which had only been released the previous day) in front of a surprised Paul McCartney and George Harrison.

Monterey Fireworks

The band then flew to the US to appear at the Monterey Pop Festival, with a line-up that epitomized the Summer of Love, featuring Jefferson Airplane, The Who, Janis Joplin, Otis Redding, The Byrds, Simon and Garfunkel, and The Mamas and the Papas. In contrast, Jimi Hendrix was completely unknown, but he seized the opportunity with an incendiary performance and stole the show.

Clad in red velvet flares, a ruffled shirt and a feather boa, he tore through the set he had perfected in the UK, including his singles and covers of Bob Dylan's 'Like a Rolling Stone' and B. B. King's

Monterey Pop Festival, June 1967

'You never told me he was *that* f***ing good.'

ERIC CLAPTON (AFTER FIRST HEARING HENDRIX PERFORM)

53

'Rock Me Baby', climaxing with The Troggs' 'Wild Thing' and the ritual burning of his guitar. The tumultuous reaction was almost drowned out by the feedback coming from the speakers.

Monkee Business

The Experience followed up with six nights at San Francisco's legendary Fillmore West and some West Coast rest and relaxation in the exalted company of David Crosby, Stephen Stills, Joni Mitchell and Mama Cass, before heading out on their first US tour. But they were on a bill with the Monkees, a mismatch so bizarre you have to suspect a plot. The Monkees' audience were screaming teenage girls who had no interest in Jimi's ground-breaking music. Furthermore, the Daughters of the American Revolution organization were apoplectic at the moral corruption of their daughters. After eight shows, the Jimi Hendrix Experience were removed from the bill. From then on, they would play their own shows in the United States.

Back In New York

The band headed to New York, where they played a number of club shows and recorded their next single, 'Burning Of The Midnight Lamp'. A densely produced song, festooned with

'The time I burned my guitar it was like a sacrifice. You sacrifice the things you love. I love my guitar.'

JIMI HENDRIX

overdubs and dominated by Jimi's latest guitar gadget, the wah-wah pedal, it was another major musical step forward.

Somewhat unwisely, Jimi renewed his friendship with Curtis Knight in New York and recorded some tracks with him, produced by Ed Chalpin, who had already dusted off the contract that Jimi had signed with him and neglected to tell Chas Chandler about. Obviously Chas was not best pleased when legal papers started flying around. Neither was he enamoured with the time Jimi was 'wasting' in the studio (the Animals had famously recorded 'House Of The Rising Sun' in one take and gone down the pub, forgetting they also had to record a B-side). But times were changing and Jimi had no shortage of engineers and tape operators eager to help him create the sounds he was looking for.

'The first shockwave was Jimi Hendrix… He came along and reset all of the rules in one evening.'

JEFF BECK

The Jimi Hendrix Experience, Heathrow Airport, August 1967

'The first time I heard "Hey Joe" ..., I ... ran out and bought the record. I didn't even have a record player.'

MARK KNOPFLER

Axis: Bold As Love was released in December 1967

Just Ask the Axis

Most of the songs on *Axis: Bold As Love*, the second Jimi Hendrix Experience album, released at the beginning of December 1967, were written and constructed in the studio. It was also recorded as an album rather than a collection of individual songs, helped by Jimi's more sophisticated use of guitar gadgetry, particularly the wah-wah pedal and the phasing techniques that dominated the album. It was designed to be played from start to finish, from the space alien tomfoolery of 'EXP'; the breezy, rhythmic 'Up From The Skies'; the vibrant, rocking 'Spanish Castle Magic'; the sublime balladry of 'Little Wing'; and the heavy grunge of 'If 6 Was 9', to the final technical wizardry of the title track, swirling into the sky above.

Axis: Bold As Love came out just six months after the band's debut album and it was immediately apparent that they had come a long way in a short time. But they had taken their fans with them. The album was a Top 5 smash in the UK and the US, joining *Are You Experienced*, which was still in both charts. In the space of a year, the Jimi Hendrix Experience had come from nowhere, recorded two hit albums and four UK hit singles, and played over 200 gigs. They were superstars in the UK and had made the breakthrough in the US –1967 was definitely the year of Jimi Hendrix.

Montagu Place, London, 1967

1968: Wild Thing

The main priority for 1968 was to make Jimi Hendrix a star in the United States. The Experience warmed up for the task with European dates in January, but it was a fractious tour. Jimi was starting to resent his 'Wild Man of Pop' image and blew a fuse in Gothenburg, Sweden, wrecking his hotel room. He spent the night in police custody followed by a court appearance, ensuring more 'Wild Man of Pop' headlines.

Conquering the US

When the American tour reached Seattle in mid-February, it was the first time Jimi had been home for seven years. The reunion with his father Al, and his new wife and step-daughter, was conducted under the gaze of the local media. The following day, Jimi showed up at his old school at 9 am to receive a diploma. Fortunately, relief was at hand, quite literally, when they played Chicago a few days later and Jimi

Paris, February 1968

was added to the celebrated Cynthia Plaster Casters' mantle-piece. Allegedly, he broke the mould.

Meanwhile, the legal case between Ed Chalpin and Jimi's UK and US record labels reached court. Chalpin had released an album of Curtis Knight with Jimi, titled *Get That Feeling*, and while the cover was ruled to be misleading, the contents were not, paving the way for a slew of more such albums. Jimi's US

'He was tough on himself, but when Jimi made a mistake, he'd turn it into something cool!' EDDIE KRAMER

Olympia, London, December 1967

label, Warner Bros, eventually settled, giving Chalpin royalties and the complete rights to another album.

On 4 April, Martin Luther King was assassinated in Memphis and the American mood darkened. Jimi dedicated his Newark show to King's memory the following day and was reportedly depressed, not just at King's death, but by the riots and wanton destruction that followed.

Jams and Friction

After the tour, Jimi settled in New York to record his next album. He established a routine of jamming at various clubs in Greenwich Village and then going on to the nearby Record Plant recording studio in the early hours, often with musicians and friends in tow. Jimi was seeking to broaden his musical horizons and many sessions were spent trying out new ideas and gadgets or continuing a jam that had started at a club.

But this was beginning to cause friction within the group. Noel was particularly suspicious of other musicians in the studio and what he saw as a dilution of the original trio. He resented being told what to play and how to play it. Plus, he was concerned about where the money was going and the unsatisfactory replies he received.

'I want to write songs about tranquility, about beautiful things.'

JIMI HENDRIX

The Jimi Hendrix Experience with members of the Byrds, the Soft Machine and the Alan Price Set, Heathrow Airport, 1968

Hallenstadion, Zurich, May 1968

Chas Chandler was also becoming frustrated at the 'wasted time' spent jamming with stoned musicians in the studio, not to mention the hangers-on crowding into the control room. But Jimi was determined to work in his own way. He enjoyed the relaxed atmosphere, even if it got too relaxed at times.

'I dig Strauss and Wagner, those cats are good, and I think they are going to form the background of my music.' JIMI HENDRIX

Chas was the first to crack, quitting midway through the sessions, not just as producer but also as manager, because he felt that he could no longer guide Jimi's career. That left Mike as Jimi's manager, but he was no more sympathetic to Jimi's methods than Chas had been. Indeed, Mike's main aim was to maximize Jimi's earnings, so Jimi found his recording sessions interrupted by concerts and festival appearances. In late May, the Experience returned to Europe for shows in Italy, Switzerland, Germany and the Woburn Festival in the UK, before returning to the US, playing arenas and open-air stadiums. Jimi did not enjoy playing such big impersonal venues, but he realized that he needed to make money in order to pursue his musical ambitions. It was during this tour that he started playing his own rendition of the American national anthem, 'The Star Spangled Banner', unaccompanied, apart from a sustained wall of feedback. It invariably generated a wild reaction from the crowd.

View from the Watchtower

Meanwhile, Jimi's record labels, impatient at the lack of new material, compiled a *Smash Hits* collection, rounding up the singles, B-sides and some album tracks. *Smash Hits* spent six months in the charts, outselling his first two albums. In early September, Jimi finally released a new single, 'All Along The Watchtower', recorded back in January, within days of hearing Dylan's original on the *John Wesley Harding* album. It featured Dave Mason on rhythm guitar (but not Noel Redding, who didn't like the song). Probably the best example of Jimi's ability to orchestrate the intricacies of a song, 'All Along The Watchtower' features one of his finest guitar solos – a blast of rock, followed by slide guitar (played with his Zippo lighter), then the wah-wah guitar sound, culminating in a swirling chord section, building a cathedral of sound. Jimi had been concerned that it was a Dylan song rather than a Hendrix song. It took a while for him

to be convinced that he'd actually made a Hendrix song out of a Dylan song. Dylan certainly loved it when he heard it. 'All Along The Watchtower' gave Jimi his first – and only – American hit single. In the UK, it reached No. 5, staying in the charts for nearly three months.

'[Jimi] managed to build this bridge between true blues guitar…and modern sounds…. He brought the two together brilliantly.'

PETE TOWNSHEND

Electric Ladyland

When *Electric Ladyland* came out in October, Jimi's recording methods were vindicated, with 16 tracks spread over a double album. The guitar effects were even more elaborate, the phasing even more rampant. The opening '… And the Gods Made Love'

with its vari-speeded drums, backwards cymbals and distorted vocals; and the dreamy 'Have You Ever Been (To Electric Ladyland)', along with 'Rainy Day, Dream Away', were Jimi's best 'sound paintings' yet. As for the jams, the 13-minute '1983 (A Merman I Should Be)' anticipated jazz fusion, while the 15-minute 'Voodoo Child' was a monumental work-out with Steve Winwood on organ and Jefferson Airplane's Jack Casady on bass (Noel Redding was missing again). The closing 'Voodoo Child (Slight Return)' was a template for heavy metal. In the US, the album went to No. 1. In the UK, where it reached No. 6, the record company commissioned a different sleeve from the one that Jimi had specifically suggested. The photograph of 21 naked ladies, posing on the gatefold sleeve, caused instant controversy, which was quite possibly the intention.

Problems Piling Up

During the Experience's West Coast tour that autumn, Jimi attended Cream's farewell tour at the Los Angeles Forum, which was a salutary reminder of the tensions within his own group. Noel Redding was already aware that his relationship with Jimi was reaching breaking point and was forming his own band, Fat Mattress. Jimi was also aware that he had significant management issues with Mike Jeffery. Jimi wanted to make music, Mike wanted to make money. This would be difficult to reconcile.

With The Experience, L'Olympia, Paris, January 1968

1969: End of the Experience

On 4 January 1969, the Jimi Hendrix Experience appeared on the BBC's *The Lulu Show*. It was prime-time Saturday evening viewing, transmitted live, and the producer insisted that Hendrix play 'Hey Joe', a song that would be familiar to the audience.

From Lulu to Woodstock

Jimi was not amused. He started with 'Voodoo Child (Slight Return)' as agreed. But when Lulu announced 'Hey Joe', Jimi launched into a blizzard of feedback. Panicked production assistants recalculated the final credits and fade-out times.

After 50 seconds, Jimi broke into the 'Hey Joe' riff and there was temporary relief until Jimi forgot the words and laughed about it. Suddenly 'Hey Joe' came to an abrupt halt and Jimi announced, 'We'd like to stop playing this rubbish and dedicate a song to Cream', ripping into 'Sunshine Of Your Love'. Cue

JH, c. 1969

'Imagination is the key to my lyrics. The rest is painted with a little science fiction.'

JIMI HENDRIX

'In a live performance, it is impossible to merely listen to what the Hendrix group does... it eats you alive.'

FRANK ZAPPA

Royal Albert Hall, London, February 1969

pandemonium. Technicians could be seen running around the back of the stage. The credits rolled and the song was rapidly faded. A furious producer told Jimi that he would never appear on BBC television again. But Jimi had had enough of playing on family entertainment TV shows.

A New Dawn?

He was also thinking beyond the Experience in interviews. He already regarded *Electric Ladyland* as in the past and was making plans for two new albums that he called *Little Band of Gypsys* and *First Rays of the New Rising Sun*. Both would come to pass, but not in the way he envisaged.

Jimi was back in London a month later for two shows at the Royal Albert Hall. Critics noted a restless nature to the shows, the band playing more like a collection of individuals than a trio. Jimi moved on to the recording studio Record Plant in New York and worked on new ideas with guitarist John McLaughlin and bassist Dave Holland who had both played on the recent ground-breaking Miles Davis albums *In A Silent Way* and *Bitches Brew*. By now even Jimi was aware that the cost of using the Record Plant as a demo studio was excessive and he and Mike Jeffery decided to build their own studio nearby that would be called Electric Lady.

The Record Plant continued to provide sanctuary during an American tour that spring. Noel Redding's new band Fat Mattress was the support act and the distance between Jimi and Noel was ominous. When the tour reached Memphis, Jimi hooked up with his army buddy Billy Cox and told him to expect a call. Then, on 3 May, while entering Canada to play a show in Toronto, customs officials found heroin and cannabis in Jimi's flight bag. He was released on $10,000 bail, but the case would hang over him for the rest of the year.

'He had monster tone, monster technique, monster songs. And soul to spare.'

KIRK HAMMETT

Experience Over

At the last gig of the tour, at Denver's Mile High Stadium on 19 June, Jimi announced that the Experience was over. Noel immediately flew back to England claiming that he had quit. Jimi and Mitch parted on good terms, however.

'My first musical epiphany probably was Jimi Hendrix, listening to "Purple Haze" on the radio.' JOE SATRIANI

Maple Leaf Gardens, Toronto, May 1969

1969: Electric Gypsy

Jimi flew to New York and announced that he would be forming a new group called the Electric Church. He made that call to bassist Billy Cox and asked him to find guitarist Larry Lee who they'd played with back in Nashville. He then added two conga players he'd come to know in Greenwich Village, Jerry Velez and Juma Sultan.

Sun and Rainbows

The new band moved to a house in upstate New York to begin rehearsals, but without a drummer, as Jimi's preferred choice, Buddy Miles, was unavailable. Returning from a break in Morocco, Jimi was approached by the organizers of an upcoming festival in Woodstock and agreed to showcase his new band under the name Gypsy Sun and Rainbows. Manager Mike Jeffery promptly moved in, to secure Jimi Hendrix as the headline act with a fee to match.

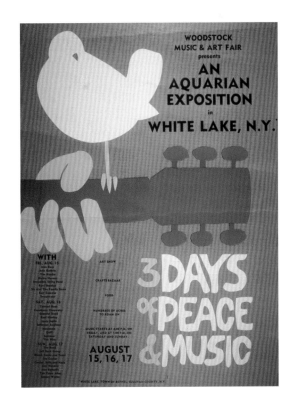

After some deliberation, Mitch Mitchell agreed to return to the drum stool, but by now time was tight and the Woodstock line-up had reached prodigious proportions with The Who, Jefferson Airplane, Janis Joplin, Sly and The Family Stone,

Santana, Joe Cocker, Ten Years After, Canned Heat and, making their debut, Crosby, Stills & Nash.

'Music makes me high on stage, and that's the truth. It's like being almost addicted to music.'

JIMI HENDRIX

Peace and Love

Over half a million people descended on the unsuspecting village of Bethel near Woodstock on 15 August, for what had been billed as 'Three Days of Peace and Music'. There was cheerful chaos until torrential rain on the second day turned the 600-acre site into a quagmire. Jimi was due to close the festival at midnight on the third day, but it was nearly 8 o'clock the following morning before he appeared on stage, in front of a gradually diminishing crowd of mud-spattered survivors and revellers.

Woodstock Music & Art Fair, August 1969

'We try to make our music so loose and hard-hitting that it hits your soul hard enough to make it open.'

JIMI HENDRIX

Woodstock Festival, August 1969

Only Jimi and Mitch had played big festival shows before. For the others, it was a daunting debut, and the set was hesitant and lacklustre until Jimi eventually took control on 'Voodoo Child (Slight Return)'. Out of the closing cacophony emerged the howling, sustained notes of 'The Star Spangled Banner', shaking everyone awake, before the feedback dissolved into the strident introduction to 'Purple Haze'.

As a performance, it was woefully under-rehearsed. Apart from Mitch and Billy Cox, the others were out of their depth. However, the subsequent Woodstock movie provided an overriding iconic image of Hendrix – dressed in a blue, fringed vest and red bandana, teasing out the notes of the American national anthem.

'...if I want to wear a red bandana and turquoise slacks and if I want my hair down to my ankles, well, that's me.' JIMI HENDRIX

Dark Days After Woodstock

Gypsy Sun and Rainbows did not last long after Woodstock. They played two more gigs in New York and then splintered. Musically it was never going to gel. The autumn of 1969 was a somewhat murky one for Jimi. There was a lot of paranoia, some of it drug-induced. There are stories of Jimi being visited by the Black Panthers at his house (the Panthers were keen to get Jimi's public support; Jimi was less keen). There are stories of Jimi being kidnapped and held hostage before being freed by manager Mike Jeffery. And there are stories of Mike's 'associates' intimidating people around Jimi.

'I started out playing guitar because Jimi Hendrix was my hero, so my roots were really based on Jimi … and his style of playing.'

JOE SATRIANI

Jimi was spending a lot of time at the Record Plant studio. But the recording sessions were often aimless, as Jimi toyed with ideas without a clear sense of direction. He completed a couple of songs and recorded a lot of blues. Meanwhile former manager Ed Chalpin was getting impatient for the album he was owed, following his settlement with Warner Bros. And Warner Bros were getting restless too; it had been a year since *Electric Ladyland* and there was no sign of a new album.

Band of Gypsys

The problems were eased when Jimi agreed to record a live album for Ed Chalpin at New York's rock venue Fillmore East at the end of the year. And he reverted to a trio, keeping Billy Cox on bass and recruiting drummer Buddy Miles who was now contractually free to join him. Mitch was happy to take a break and returned to the UK. Now the sessions at the Record Plant had a focus and Jimi prepared new material with the Band of Gypsys, as he'd dubbed them. December was spent rehearsing, apart from a three-day break while Jimi flew to Toronto to face trial for possession of heroin and marijuana. He was acquitted of both charges by the jury after an eight-hour deliberation. Jimi's mood dramatically improved afterwards.

1970:
Freedom

On the evening of 31 December 1969, the Band of Gypsys played the first of four sets at the Fillmore East over two days. They were some of the most focused live performances Jimi gave.

'And with the music we will paint pictures of Earth and space so that the listener can be taken somewhere.'

JIMI HENDRIX

Berkeley Community Theatre, California, May 1970

Set For The Seventies

He utilized the dynamic of his new rhythm section to the full, using four effects pedals: a wah-wah pedal, a customized Octavia box, a Fuzz Face distortion unit and a UniVibe flutter pedal. That gave him a wider range of sounds than he'd had before. There was plenty to focus on and little room for grandstanding or flash pyrotechnics. The majority of the songs had not been released by the Experience and those that had been were given a facelift. It was dawn on 2 January when they finished the fourth set. The feeling in and around Jimi was almost euphoric. At last there seemed to be a direction to follow. Jimi was set for the Seventies.

'[Jimi] was doing his own thing instead of what was expected of black musicians at the time.'

TRACY CHAPMAN

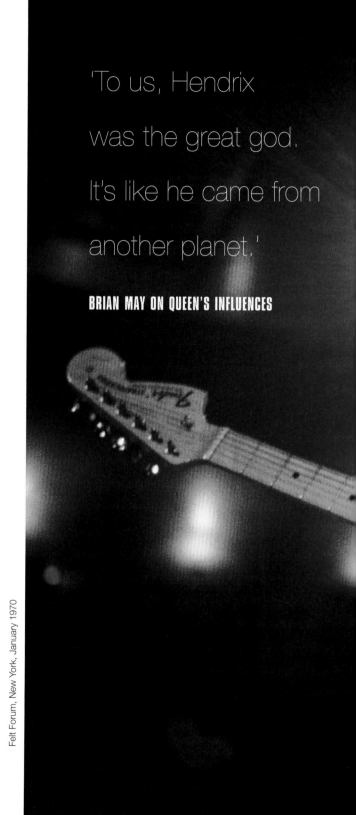

'To us, Hendrix was the great god. It's like he came from another planet.'

BRIAN MAY ON QUEEN'S INFLUENCES

Felt Forum, New York, January 1970

Cal Expo, April 1970

Gypsys Disbanded

By the third week of January 1970, Jimi had picked and mixed the tracks for the *Band of Gypsys* album with engineer Eddie Kramer. On 28 January, the band made another New York appearance at Madison Square Garden, as part of the Winter Festival for Peace, alongside Harry Belafonte; Blood, Sweat and Tears; The Rascals; and Dave Brubeck. After struggling through two songs, it was obvious that Jimi, who had been uncharacteristically silent before the show, was in bad shape. He walked off saying, 'I'm sorry, we just can't get it together.' A bad acid trip has been blamed. There may have been other issues. Whatever, the Band of Gypsys was over.

'The Band of Gypsys was a group about growth, evolution without ego or interference.'

BILLY COX

Re-Experienced

Jimi retreated to the studio again. Finding musicians to record with was not a problem. Keeping his manager Mike Jeffery at bay was. Mike began making plans for a major American tour – although he left gaps to ensure that the next album got finished. There was speculation that the Experience was about to reform. This increased when Jimi went to London for a few days in March. Mitch was amenable to returning, but Jimi's relationship with Noel had deteriorated beyond repair. Instead he stuck by Billy Cox.

The Cry Of Love tour started in California in late April. Several new songs were incorporated into the set, including some that had been played by the Band of Gypsys. Some of the older songs were now used as a launchpad for extended jamming. The playing was generally good and the audiences were enthusiastic. And they were billed as the Jimi Hendrix Experience again, so the money was good.

Electric Lady

The *Band of Gypsys* album had been released near the start of the tour and was making its way up the US charts towards the Top Five. It would do the same in the UK later that summer. Recording sessions were becoming more productive as well. In June, Jimi moved into his newly completed Electric Lady studio in Greenwich Village. Now nobody could complain about the cost of being in the studio any more. The downside was that Jimi was either in the studio, on stage or in between the two. He was becoming drained, and his rock'n'roll lifestyle was not helping. He could generally get it up for live shows, but in the studio it was getting harder to ignite the sparks.

'I don't want to be a clown any more. I don't want to be a rock'n'roll star.'

JIMI HENDRIX

The End

After a mammoth pay-day at the Atlanta International Pop Festival in front of 200,000 people in early July, Jimi hoped he would be allowed to finish the album undisturbed, but more dates kept piling up. Some of them were not very well organized either; at the New York Pop Festival, they had to contend with local radio stations coming through the speakers.

1970: Hear My Train A Comin'

At the end of July, the Experience flew out to Hawaii to take part in the Rainbow Bridge film project that was notable for the absence of a script or a plot.

The End Of The Rainbow

The project appeared to hinge on a Jimi Hendrix gig on the picturesque slopes of Haleakala mountain on Maui, along with any other ideas that might strike the filmmakers. These ideas did not include telling the locals about the gig and only about 400 showed up.

'Blues is easy to play, but hard to feel.'

JIMI HENDRIX

Billy Cox, Isle of Wight Festival, August 1970

'Jimi Hendrix changed my life. Each generation influences the following one and as a consequence brings it back to the past.' ROBERT SMITH

Isle of Wight Festival, August 1970

Afterwards, Jimi flew straight back to New York to sort out the songs for the next album. But already there was a British show at the Isle of Wight Festival booked for the end of August and more European dates to follow.

Isle of Wight

Jimi arrived in London two days before his Isle of Wight show, visibly exhausted from a hectic month at Electric Lady pulling songs together and the after-effects of a very stoned party to celebrate the official opening of the studio. Although the three-day festival was now in its third year, the 1970 festival was particularly chaotic because around 600,000 people had made their way on to the island, many of whom were ticket-less and planned to gatecrash. There was also financial uncertainty surrounding the event. As the headlining act, Jimi found himself going on at 3 am.

Even as he waited to go on stage, there were technical problems with the equipment. Jimi opened with the British National Anthem, 'God Save The Queen', in his own inimitable style, but the planned follow-up – a romp through 'Sgt Pepper's Lonely Hearts Club Band' – fell flat when Mitch's introduction turned into an impromptu drum solo as Jimi's amp went on the blink. They tried to drown out the sound hassles with forceful versions

of 'Spanish Castle Magic' and 'All Along The Watchtower', but when they settled into the slower intricacies of 'Machine Gun', they were disrupted by the conversations from the festival security walkie talkies coming through the PA.

Crowd Pleaser

They continued on regardless, mixing new and unreleased songs with old favourites from their first album, and Jimi even reverted to some of his wilder stage antics that had largely been phased out in an attempt to keep the crowd happy. The technical gremlins had largely abated by the time they got to the closing trio of 'Hey Joe', 'Purple Haze' and 'Voodoo Child (Slight Return)'. Finally, after another drum solo, Jimi finished the two-hour show with another new song, 'In From The Storm', tossed his guitar to the floor and walked off. It was a disjointed show, plagued by sound problems, but with moments of Hendrix genius shining through.

Too Much

There was little time to brood, however. They were flown straight out to Sweden and 15 hours later Jimi was back on stage at Gröna Lund in Stockholm. The next day, they played Gothenburg

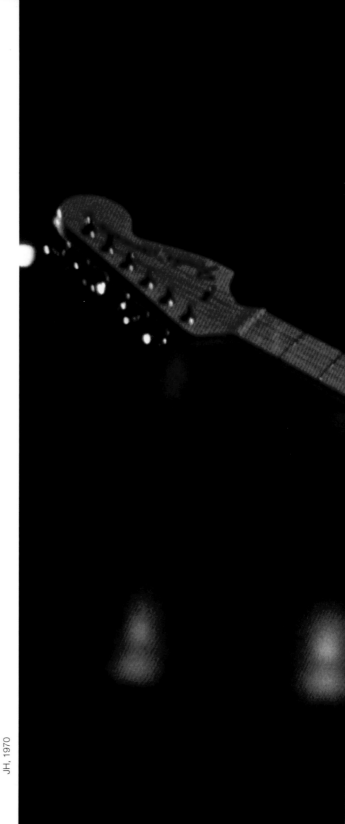

JH, 1970

Last concert: Love + Peace Festival, Isle of Fehmarn, Germany, 6 September 1970

and the day after that Arhus, Denmark. Jimi finally succumbed to exhaustion, compounded by a cold and high temperature, and left the stage after just three songs. But Jimi was not the only casualty; Billy Cox had apparently been dosed with Phencyclidine (PCP) and was suffering from psychosis and paranoia.

No Love, No Peace

The band limped through shows in Copenhagen and Berlin, making six shows in six days, before travelling to the Isle of Fehmarn on the northern coast of Germany on 5 September to play the inappropriately named Love + Peace Festival. By the evening, high winds and rain made the stage unplayable and Jimi's spot was rescheduled for the following day. Meanwhile, the mood among the crowd turned ugly after violent clashes between biker gangs. The Experience played on 6 September, initially to boos from the crowd, and the atmosphere remained intimidating throughout.

They flew straight to London, where Billy Cox received medical treatment for acute psychosis, and was then flown back to the US to recover. The remaining tour dates in France and Italy were cancelled. Jimi was due to return to New York to finish off the album but seemed reluctant to leave. He remained in London,

'I'm the one that has to die.
When it's time for me to
die. So let me live my life,
the way I want to.'

JIMI HENDRIX

visiting friends and jamming with the funk band Eric Burdon and War at Ronnie Scott's club.

Sleeping Pill Overdose

On the night of 17 September, Jimi stayed with a girlfriend, Monika Dannemann, at the Samarkand Hotel in Bayswater, London. The following day, an ambulance was summoned to the hotel at 11.18 am. It arrived at 11.27 am and departed again at 11.45 am. Jimi Hendrix was pronounced dead on arrival at St Mary Abbot's Hospital. His death was officially recorded at 12.45 pm. At the inquest, on 28 September, the pathologist reported that Jimi's death was due to inhalation of vomit due to barbiturate intoxication. No other drugs were reported and no needle marks were found.

'Will I live tomorrow? / Well
I just can't say / But I know
for sure / I don't live today.'

JIMI HENDRIX

Aftermath

J imi Hendrix's body was flown back to Seattle, Washington, where he was buried on 1 October at Greenwood Memorial Park in Renton, after a funeral service at the Dunlap Baptist Church, where Jimi's aunt had played the organ when he was a child. It was attended by Mitch Mitchell and Noel Redding, Eddie Kramer, Buddy Miles, Johnny Winter and Miles Davis among others, together with Jimi's family.

'When I die, just keep on playing the records.'

JIMI HENDRIX

What Happened Next

Jimi left no will, so his estate passed to his father Al Hendrix. Initial reports were that the estate might be worth as little as $500,000, and it was alleged that only $20,000 could be

In his Mayfair flat, 1969, once the residence of George Frederick Handel

L–R: Betty Mabry, Miles Davis, Devon Wilson (JH long-time friend), 1 October 1970

found in his bank accounts. It quickly became apparent that Jimi's business affairs were in a labyrinthine state of confusion. He had signed contracts with production companies and management companies who had in turn signed contracts with other companies. Al was recommended to Leo Branton, a lawyer who was handling Nat King Cole's estate on behalf of his widow, who began unravelling some of the strands of Jimi's complex affairs.

At the time of his death, Jimi was completing his next studio album. He had given it a title – *First Rays Of The New Rising Sun* – and there was a provisional track listing scribbled on a tape box. In addition, there were hundreds of hours of recordings – songs, jams, fragments – made over the previous three years, and countless live recordings of performances from across his career.

'I consider [Jimi] to be a musician, a great, great musician.'

B.B. KING

'He was very self-effacing about his music but then when he picked up that guitar he was just a monster.' **PAUL MCCARTNEY**

Cry Of Love

Mitch Mitchell and engineer Eddie Kramer went into the studio in late 1970 to work on the tracks that were closest to completion. *The Cry Of Love* album, released in March 1971, went Top Three in the UK and US. But subsequent releases were more about cashing in on the Hendrix legacy rather than enhancing it. To make matters worse, there were a growing number of unauthorized releases falsely claiming to feature Jimi playing, such as with Little Richard, the Isley Brothers or whoever, before he came to the UK in 1967.

Meanwhile, the search for the Hendrix 'missing millions' was being blocked at every turn. His UK royalties had been frozen in an interminable court case involving Ed Chalpin. The rest of his income remained trapped behind an impenetrable thicket of companies, mostly registered in tax havens. Any chance of recovering Jimi's money was effectively lost when manager Mike Jeffery was killed in a plane crash over France in 1973.

Crash Landing

In 1974, lawyer Leo Branton sold the Hendrix music catalogue to a Panamanian tax shelter called PMSA. They hired Alan

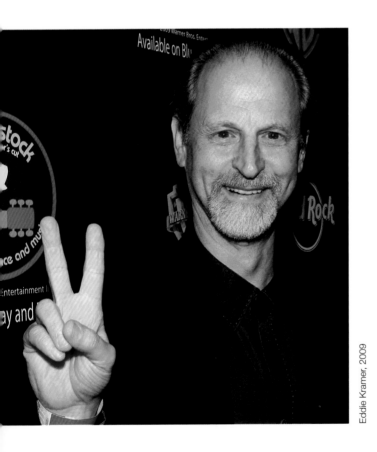

Eddie Kramer, 2009

Douglas, a producer who'd worked with Hendrix in his last year, to overhaul the catalogue. Douglas started sifting through the 600 hours of tapes Jimi had left behind and released *Crash Landing*, featuring some excellent Hendrix studio jams – except that the other musicians had been erased and replaced by overdubbed session musicians. Critics and fans denounced it as cultural vandalism.

By the end of the Seventies, Jimi was no longer hot commercial property. *The Essential Jimi Hendrix* compilation in 1979 failed to chart. The advent of the CD in the mid-Eighties could have been an opportunity to revive Hendrix's legend, but it was wasted because the CDs used inferior versions of the original master tapes and were of poor sound quality.

'I learned from Jimi Hendrix. They all wanted him to do the tricks, and at the end of his career, he just wanted to play.' PRINCE

Mike Jeffery, JH's manager

It took a Wrangler jeans TV commercial in 1990 using 'Crosstown Traffic' as its soundtrack to make Hendrix sound relevant. Hastily released as a single, the song crept into the charts, but a *Cornerstones* compilation later that year was a Top Five album and provided the impetus to overhaul the Hendrix catalogue. By 1993, Hendrix was reckoned to be selling a million albums a year. After discovering that MCA Records was preparing to pay $40 million for the US rights to Jimi's recordings, Al Hendrix sued Leo Branton, claiming that he had mismanaged the Jimi Hendrix estate and tricked him into selling the rights. The case was eventually settled out of court in 1995 and Al Hendrix regained control of Jimi's estate. He set up Experience Hendrix to manage the estate and put his daughter Janie in charge. Mitch Mitchell, Billy Cox and engineer Eddie Kramer were brought in to oversee the remastering of Jimi's catalogue from the original tapes.

First Rays

In 1997, the 'missing' album, *First Rays Of The New Rising Sun*, was released. The album's 17 tracks were chosen from scribbled notes Jimi had left, plus the recollections of Mitch, Billy and Eddie, who were there at the time. Al Hendrix died in 2002, leaving control of Experience Hendrix to his daughter Janie – Jimi's half-sister. She has gradually brought order to the previous chaos of the Jimi Hendrix catalogue.

JH inducted into Rock & Roll Hall of Fame (Al Hendrix, right), 1992

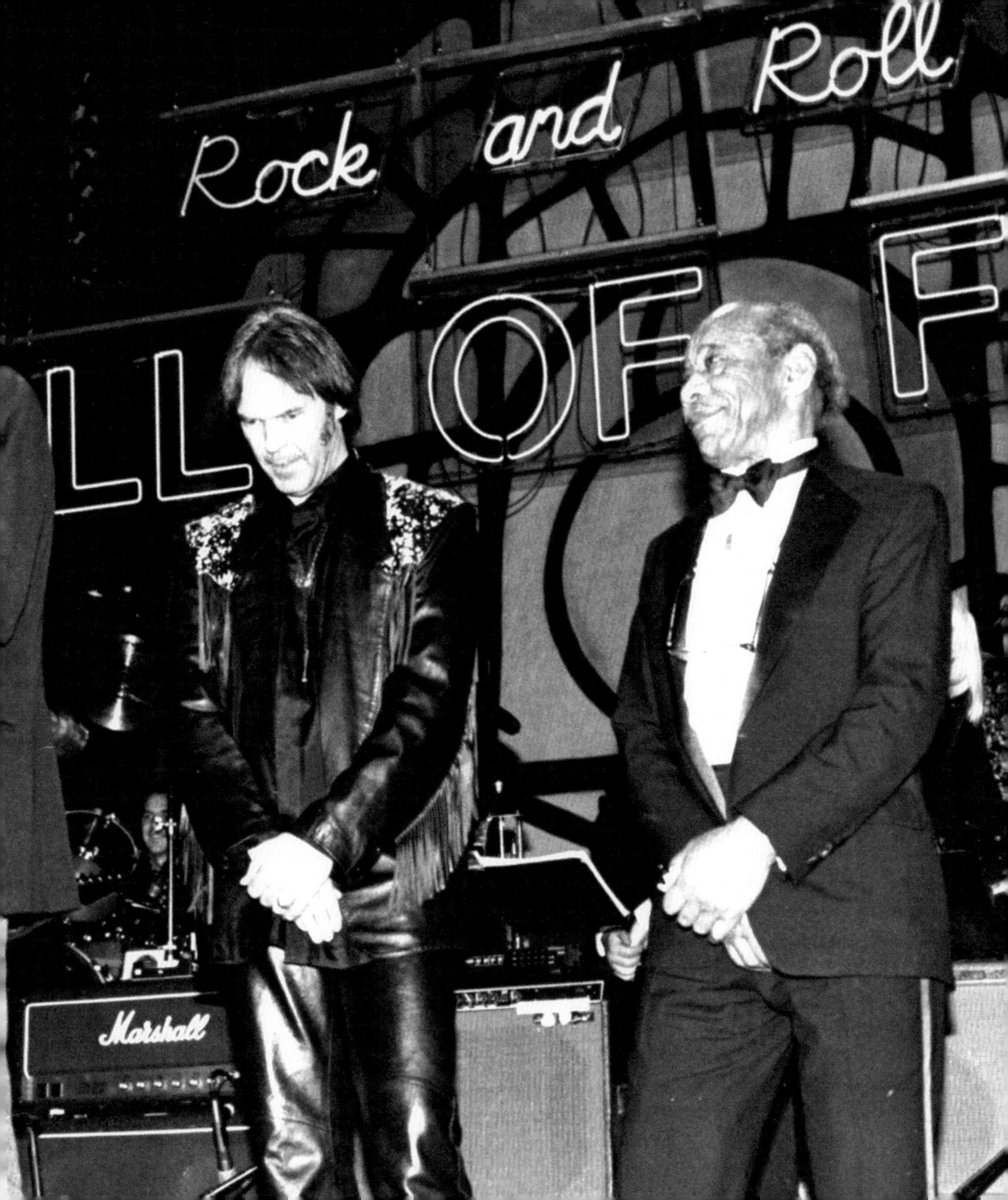
Rock and Roll
LL OF F
Marshall

Buying Hendrix

There is nothing, repeat nothing, that Jimmy James recorded that gives any insight into what Jimi Hendrix became after he arrived in England in September 1966.

Pre-1967

There are dozens of albums purporting to feature Hendrix with Lonnie Youngblood, Little Richard or other people he played with. Any information on the sleeve is usually misleading or false. Hendrix does not even appear on many of the recordings; sometimes a session guitarist has overdubbed a Hendrix-style part. And it would take an expert to pick him out on most of the tracks that he does play on.

The Studio Albums

The three studio albums that Jimi Hendrix released during his life – *Are You Experienced*, *Axis: Bold As Love* and *Electric Ladyland* – remain the essential monuments to his legend.

'I don't think there's any music that you hear on the radio today that would be possible without Jimi Hendrix.' JOE BONAMASSA

The Jimi Hendrix Experience, c. 1967

Are You Experienced now contains Jimi's first three single – 'Hey Joe', 'Purple Haze' and 'The Wind Cries Mary' – and their B-sides, so there is no need to buy a Greatest Hits collection. *Axis: Bold As Love* and *Electric Ladyland* were both sequenced to be heard as a complete album.

First Rays Of The New Rising Sun is the fourth essential studio album. It does not compare to the first three, because most of the songs had not been completed and nobody knows how Jimi would have finished them off. The 17 tracks were recorded during a confused period in Jimi's life and the title indicates that this is the beginning of a new musical phase. The other essential studio album is *BBC Sessions* that rounds up 27 tracks Hendrix recorded for various BBC TV and radio shows during 1967, offering an illuminating insight into the band during their first epic year together. It includes the odd Elvis, Bob Dylan and Beatles cover and a spontaneous Radio One jingle, plus the complete *Lulu Show* experience from 1969.

If the other studio albums don't rank as essential, they are not without interest. *South Saturn Delta* rounds up the best of what didn't make it on to either *Electric Ladyland* or *First Rays Of The New Rising Sun*. And *Blues* hones in on Jimi's endless fascination with the 12-bar. The other releases and multiple CD sets are mainly for collectors who wish to delve deeper into Hendrix.

Live Albums

An extraordinary number of Jimi Hendrix concerts were recorded, either by professional sound engineers and film crews, or taken from the mixing desk, taped off the TV or radio or by audience members. It would probably be easier to list the shows that were not recorded rather than the ones that were. Experience Hendrix have released several major Hendrix shows and have an ongoing release schedule. They have also set up an 'authorized bootleg' label called Dagger.

Electric Ladyland was released in October 1968

The three major festivals that Jimi played – Monterey in 1967, Woodstock in 1969 and the Isle of Wight in 1970 – were all recorded and filmed. Of these, *Jimi Plays Monterey* is the best, catching the essence of the Jimi Hendrix Experience as they catapulted their way to stardom. *Live At Woodstock*, the most famous show Hendrix played, and the epoch-defining moment when he appropriates 'The Star Spangled Banner' followed by 'Purple Haze', still raises goose bumps. But the 75 minutes that precede it are a real test of stamina for even the most devoted Hendrix fan. *Live At The Isle Of Wight,* now re-titled *Blue Wild Angel*, has tended to be maligned over the years, because of the sound problems that bedevilled the gig and Jimi's own state of mind, but the now-unedited, two-hour show features seven songs that were lined up for his next album.

Of the other significant gigs, *Band Of Gypsys* is now available as the 2-CD *Live At The Fillmore East*, featuring sizeable chunks of the four sets of rock/funk crossover that Jimi played with Buddy Miles and Billy Cox, including three versions of 'Machine Gun'. *Live At Berkeley*, recorded at the small Berkeley Community Theater in May 1970, while hundreds of ticket-less fans caused mayhem outside trying to get in, is a fine example of Jimi channelling all his pent-up emotions into one great gig, mixing new and old songs into a seamless torrent. And *Freedom: Atlanta Pop Festival* a couple of months later is almost as good, albeit on a far grander scale.

The Guitar God

Fifty years from Jimi Hendrix's premature death, his legacy burns as pervasively as ever. The music he recorded during his brief four-year career is as relevant now as it was then. Much of it still sounds ground-breaking.

The Legacy

Many of his songs are around the three-four minute mark and yet they retain an epic quality. The three studio albums he released during his brief four-year career trace a remarkable trajectory and the album he was working on when he died – finally put together as close to his wishes as possible in 1997 – still hints at the direction he might have followed if he had lived.

'Jimi was an absolute original. You don't hear that kind of soul today.' DON HENLEY

JH, 1970

'Everybody else just screwed it up, and thought wailing away [on guitar] is the answer. But it ain't; you've got to be a Jimi to do that, you've got to be one of the special cats.' KEITH RICHARDS

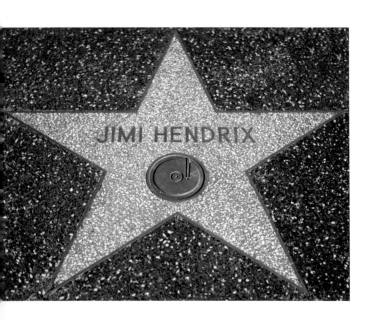

After a quarter of a century of artless exploitation and mismanagement, Jimi's voluminous catalogue – it is vast – now has a semblance of order; most bands these days would be happy to release a couple of albums in four years. Regular compilations and live albums continue to shine a light on different aspects of Jimi's musical character. *Valleys Of Neptune* in 2010 and *People, Hell And Angels* in 2013 both made the US Top Five.

Covered

Jimi's songs live south on, not just in his records but in countless versions performed by other artists to whom he continues to cast an almost mesmeric spell. Eric Clapton, who comes as close as any to equalling Jimi's influence, played a reverential cover of 'Little Wing' on his 2016 album, *Live in San Diego With JJ Cale*. It was the latest in a string of live versions he recorded, since he first covered the song on Derek and the Dominos' *Layla And Other Assorted Love Songs*, just a week before Jimi died. It features on his 2008 reunion album with Steve Winwood, *Live From Madison Square Garden*, alongside a 16-minute version of 'Voodoo Child' with Winwood, reprising the part he played on Jimi's original recording.

Musicians' Musician

It is not just Jimi's contemporaries who are obsessed with him. Slash famously introduced Guns N' Roses' 'Civil War' on their early 1990s tour with the riff from 'Voodoo Child (Slight Return)', which is now widely considered the rock'n'roll national anthem. The elusive Frank Ocean, regarded by many as the finest living soul singer-songwriter, has nominated 'Crosstown Traffic' as his favourite ever song.

'It's funny how people love the dead; once you're dead, you're made for life.'

JIMI HENDRIX

'I've been imitated so well, I've heard people copy my mistakes.' **JIMI HENDRIX**

That was also the song that Living Colour, who did more than most to blow down musical barriers in the 1990s, chose to cover on the Jimi Hendrix tribute album, *Stone Free*, in 1993. The list of contributing artists on that album included The Cure, Spin Doctors, Body Count, Nigel Kennedy, P.M. Dawn, Belly, M.A.C.C. (made up of Mike McCready and Jeff Ament from Pearl Jam with Chris Cornell and Mike Cameron from Soundgarden), as well as Slash teaming up with Paul Rodgers and Buddy Miles and Billy Cox from the Band Of Gypsys. That's in addition to the expected

JH, 1967

123

list of suspects like Eric Clapton, Jeff Beck, Buddy Guy and Pat Metheny. It would be hard to find a broader list of musicians all under the influence of one man.

Slight (But Continuous) Return

Beyond the innumerable covers of Jimi's songs, and the direct influence his playing has had on every rock guitarist of note since, is a subconscious influence that has impacted on guitarists the world over. Jimi was not just a pioneer of the guitar, he was also a musical sponge who soaked up music from any source and then squeezed it out of his guitar, pushing the limits of the instrument into jazz, funk, noise and ambient rock. And it's not even as if he was conscious of the different genres of music that he was moving into. The sounds he produced were just natural expressions of his character.

To give just one example, because Jimi was left-handed, he would re-string a right-handed guitar to suit him. This meant that the upper and middle strings had a mellower sound. This sound has been widely adopted since, notably by Prince, Stevie Ray Vaughan and John Frusciante of the Red Hot Chili Peppers.

The flame that Jimi Hendrix lit is unlikely to be extinguished any time soon.

Felt Forum, New York, January 1970

Further Information

Jimi Hendrix Vital Info

Birth Name:	James Marshall Hendrix
Born:	27 November 1942; Seattle, USA
Died:	18 September 1970; London, UK
Role:	Guitarist, singer, songwriter, producer

Discography

Jimi Hendrix In The Charts

- Jimi Hendrix's chart career is not spectacular. He had only one No. 1 album in the US and one No. 1 single in the UK. His highest single placing in the US was No. 20.

- His music was not radio-friendly, but it has lasted far longer and had more impact than most of his contemporaries with more impressive chart statistics.

- In his brief career Hendrix released just three studio albums and one live album.

- Since his death there have been nearly 100 releases from the hundreds of hours of unreleased studio recordings and concert recordings, as well as compilations.

- He continues to sell around a million albums a year across his extensive catalogue, which is a better indication of his real influence than his chart perfomance.

Chart Summary

UK Albums
No. 1s:	0
Top 10s:	13
Weeks in Top 10:	58
Top 40s:	29
Weeks in Top 40:	205

UK Singles
No. 1s:	1
Weeks at No 1:	1
Top 10s:	5
Weeks in Top 10:	58
Top 40s:	9
Weeks in Top 40:	64

US Albums
No. 1s:	1
Weeks at No. 1:	2
Top 10s:	10
Top 200s:	49
Weeks in Top 200:	584

US Singles
No. 1s:	0
Top 10s:	0
Top 40s:	1
Top 100s:	7
Weeks in Top 100:	48

Studio Albums

Release	Title	US chart position	Weeks in chart	UK chart position	Weeks in chart
1967	Are You Experienced	5	77	2	34
1967	Axis: Bold As Love	3	13	5	16
1968	Electric Ladyland	1	17	6	12
1971	Cry Of Love	3	17	2	14
1971	Rainbow Bridge	15	9	16	8
1972	War Heroes	48	18	23	3
1972	Rare Hendrix	82	11	-*	-
1974	Loose Ends	-	-	-	-
1975	Crash Landing	5	9	35	-
1975	Midnight Lightning	43	11	46	1
1980	Nine To The Universe	127	7	-	-
1989	Radio One	119	17	30	6
1994	Blues	45	18	10	4
1995	Voodoo Soup	66	7	83	1
1997	First Rays Of The New Rising Sun	49	13	37	3
1997	South Saturn Delta	51	6	-	-
1998	BBC Sessions	50	9	42	4
2010	Valleys Of Neptune	4	15	21	6
2013	People, Hell And Angels	2	11	30	3

* If no figure given, record either was not released in that territory or did not chart

Live Albums

Release	Title	US chart position	Weeks in chart	UK chart position	Weeks in chart
1970	Band Of Gypsys	5	23	6	30
1970	Monterey International Pop Festival (US only, with Otis Redding)	16	20	-	-
1971	Experience (UK only)	-	-	9	6
1971	Jimi Hendrix At The Isle Of Wight	-	-	17	2
1972	Hendrix In The West	12	9	7	14
1973	Soundtrack Recordings From The Film Jimi Hendrix	89	18	37	1
1982	The Jimi Hendrix Concerts	79	8	16	11
1986	Jimi Plays Monterey	192	3	-	-
1987	Jimi Plays Winterland	-	-	-	-
1994	Woodstock	37.	8	32	3
1996	Message To Love: The Isle Of Wight Festival	-	-	-	-
1999	Live At The Fillmore East	65	4	87	1
1999	Live At Woodstock	90	3	76	1
2002	Blue Wild Angel: Live At The Isle Of Wight	200	1	-	-
2003	Live At Berkeley	191	1	-	-
2007	Live At Monterey	123	2	-	-
2011	Winterland	49	2	92	1
2013	Miami Pop Festival	39	2	-	-
2014	Live At Monterey	123	2	-	-
2015	Freedom: Atlanta Pop Festival	63	3	87	1
2016	Machine Gun – The Fillmore East Show	66	2	80	1

Compilations

Release	Title	US chart position	Weeks in chart	UK chart position	Weeks in chart
1968	Smash Hits	6	17	4	25
1975	Jimi Hendrix (UK only compilation)	-	-	35	4
1978	The Essential Jimi Hendrix (US-only compilation)	114	15	-	-
1979	The Essential Jimi Hendrix Vol. II	156	7	-	-
1984	Kiss The Sky	148		-	-
1990	Cornerstones 1967-1970 (UK only)	-	-	5	16
1991	Lifelines: The Jimi Hendrix Story (US only)	174	2	-	-
1992	The Ultimate Experience	72	77	25	31
1997	Experience Hendrix – The Best Of (UK-only compilation)	-	-	18	19
2000	Experience Hendrix – The Best Of	133	52	10	9
2000	The Jimi Hendrix Experience	78	3	-	-
2002	Voodoo Child – The Collection	112	4	10	15
2007	Experience Hendrix – The Best Of (UK-only compilation)	-	-	88	4
2010	Fire – The Collection	-	-	29	3
2010	West Coast Seattle Boy: The Jimi Hendrix Anthology	153	1	-	-
2018	Both Sides Of The Sky	8	4	8	2
2018	Experience Hendrix – The Best Of	-	-	69	4

Singles

Release*	Title	US chart position	Weeks in chart	UK chart position	Weeks in chart
Dec 1966	'Hey Joe'	-	-	6	11
Mar/Jun 1967	'Purple Haze'	65	8	3	14
May/Jun 1967	'The Wind Cries Mary'	-	-	6	11
Aug 1967	'Burning Of The Midnight Lamp'	-	-	18	9
Nov 1967	'Foxey Lady' (US only)	67	4	-	-
Feb 1968	'Up From The Skies' (US only)	82	4	-	-
Sept (US)/ Oct (UK) 1968	'All Along The Watchtower'	20	9	5	12
Nov 1968 (US)/ Apr 1969 (UK)	'Crosstown Traffic'	52	8	37	3
Oct 1970	'Voodoo Chile'	-	-	1	13
Mar 1971	'Freedom'	59	8	-	-
Mar 1971	'Angel'	-	-	-	-
Oct 1971 (US)	'Dolly Dagger'/ 'The Star Spangled Banner'	74	7	-	-
Oct 1971	'Gypsy Eyes'/'Remember'	-	-	35	5
Apr 1972	'Johnny B. Goode'	-	-	35.	5
Apr 1990	'Crosstown Traffic'	-	-	61	5
Oct 1990	'All Along The Watchtower'	-	-	52	3

* UK release date given first, unless otherwise stated

Official Bootlegs

Dagger Records, owned by Experience Hendrix, has released a number of albums 'that don't meet the technical standard for mainstream release':

1998	Live At Oakland Coliseum (1969)
1999	Live At Clark University (1968)
2000	Morning Symphony Ideas (studio tracks, 1969–70)
2001	Live In Ottawa (1968)
2002	Baggy's Rehearsal Sessions (Band Of Gypsys sessions, 1969)
2003	Paris 1967/San Francisco 1968
2004	Hear My Music (studio tracks, 1969)
2005	Live At The Isle Of Fehmarn (1970)
2006	Burning Desire (Band Of Gypsys sessions, 1969/70)
2008	Live In Paris And Ottawa (1968)
2009	Live At Woburn (1968)
2012	Live In Cologne (1969)

Most-Covered Hendrix Songs

- 'Little Wing'
- 'Voodoo Child (Slight Return)'
- 'Red House'
- 'Angel'
- 'Crosstown Traffic'

Awards (Selected)

Melody Maker
1967 Pop Musician Of The Year

Disc & Music Echo
1968 World Top Musician

Hollywood Walk Of Fame
1991 Star on Hollywood Boulevard

Rock & Roll Hall Of Fame
1992 Inducted

Grammys
1992 Lifetime Achievement Award

English Heritage
1997 Blue Plaque unveiled at Hendrix's apartment, 23 Brook Street, London

UK Music Hall Of Fame
2005 Inducted

Library Of Congress
2005 *Are You Experienced* added to National Recording Registry

Rolling Stone Magazine
2011 Greatest Guitarist Of All Time

Rhythm & Blues Hall Of Fame
2019 Band of Gypsys inducted

Streams

Experience Hendrix has a number of free concert streams available on its website: www.jimihendrix.com

Denver 1968	New York 1969
Dallas 1968	Denver 1969
Houston 1968	Los Angeles 1970
Chicago 1968	Tulsa 1970
Frankfurt 1969	Baltimore 1970

Biographies

Hugh Fielder (Author)

Hugh Fielder saw Jimi Hendrix six times in 1967. He was that good. The closest he came to him was when he found himself standing next to him in the toilets at London's UFO Club. Jimi was wearing velvet trousers that had no flies, which involved revealing more than was strictly appropriate. Hugh has written books on the Beatles, Pink Floyd, Led Zeppelin, Queen, Genesis, the Police, punk rock and Lady Gaga. But he is still introduced by one friend to his mates as 'the man who saw Jimi Hendrix's ....'.

Paul Du Noyer (Foreword)

Paul Du Noyer has written about music for over 30 years. He began his career as a reporter on the *NME*, went on to edit *Q* magazine and then launched *MOJO*. With hundreds of interviews to his credit he's been face to face with Madonna, Bruce Springsteen, David Bowie and Amy Winehouse. His most recent book is *Conversations With McCartney*.

Picture Credits